Benjamin D. Author

i Hope

*A Daddy's Dream
A Daughter's Wish*

ISBN: 978-1-7339949-0-3
© 2019 by Benjamin D. Author

Scripture quotations marked (NLT) are taken from the Holy Bible, New Living Translation, copyright ©1996, 2004, 2015 by Tyndale House Foundation. Used by permission of Tyndale House Publishers, Carol Stream, Illinois 60188. All rights reserved.

Scripture taken from the New King James Version®. Copyright © 1982 by Thomas Nelson. Used by permission. All rights reserved.

Cover Design by Great Lineage Publishing
www.greatlineagebooks.com

Interior Layout Design
www.PricelessDigitalMedia.com

Dedication

I dedicate this book to four of the smartest and most beautiful girls in the world -- my daughters. Daddy wants you to know that he believes in you and loves you more than life itself. I also dedicate this book to my sister, Alicia. She was the first person I watched go from a girl to a woman.

Finally, I dedicate this book to you, the reader, the girl who is blooming into a young lady. I want you to be prepared for the world that you are about to encounter. My prayer is that you realize that there's more to life than what's on TV or in your phone. So, as we go through these next 10 chapters, I want you to turn off the TV, place your phone or tablet on the charger, and be ready to explore the hopes of a Dad.

Table of Contents

Introduction 6

i Hope You Know 9

i Hope You Don't 21

i Hope You Hope 29

i Hope You Believe 37

i Hope You See 45

i Hope You Grow 61

i Hope You Love 69

i Hope You Understand 77

i Hope You See What I See 87

i Hope You Be 95

Conclusion 96

Introduction

My name is Benjamin D. Author. I am a father of five beautiful children, four girls and a boy. Currently, their ages range from 12 to 21. As a father, I've noticed that communication is key when it comes to raising children and connecting with people. It's not always what you say but how you say it that is the main ingredient to good communication.

Statistics say that women tend to express themselves better than men, and that is why I decided to write this book -- to bridge the gap between Daddy and daughter by explaining why dads have such a hard time expressing themselves to their daughters when it comes to topics of boys, sex, feelings, and other subjects that make us cringe when we hear them. I desire to tell my daughters and others like them how great they are and how great a future I hope they have, but I also want to explain to them the difficulties that I and other dads like me have when it comes to explaining our true hopes and dreams for our daughters. Every man wants his daughters to be successful, but regrettably, not every man knows how to tell them.

iHope is both personal and informational, and it contains a lot of truth-bearing, reality-sharing, and daddy-explaining of reasons why. Get away from any distraction, and be ready to read.

For I know the plans I have for you," says the Lord. "They are plans for good and not for disaster, to give you a future and a hope. Jeremiah 29:11 (NLT)

CHAPTER 1

Hope You Know

A DAD'S HOPE FOR HIS DAUGHTER TO KNOW

Being the father of four beautiful daughters, I've learned a thing or two about girls, and one of the things I've learned is that if they don't have a positive view of themselves, it's easier for them to accept how the world sees them and act accordingly. In spite of how a girl may see herself, her parents and their relationship, and even her dad, her dad wants her to know how to be different. The first time any man looks at his little girl, he sees a sight that gives him an emotion that words can't explain. He wants her to know that she is special because that is how he sees her.

The first time I laid eyes on my firstborn after the doctor had delivered her, I sat there in awe of this fragile child that was mine. I looked at her and stared, almost as if I was in a daydream. The feeling I had was like no other

I had experienced before. I handed her back to either her mom or the nurse — I can't remember – and I walked away thinking, what am I going to do? The reality of being a dad was beginning to sink in, and I was thinking:

» How am I going to do this?

» How am I going to protect her?

» If I protect her, will I be hurting her more than helping her?

All I could see was how the world would love to snatch my baby up and use her as its own. Fear, doubt, worry, pride, and a small amount of hatred were brewing up inside of me. My baby is going to be in a world that will hate her if she decides to be a good girl. Not too many women make it in this world hurt-free. My solution was that if I could be with her every step of the way, I would know that she could make it.

So many thoughts can go through a man's head when he finds out that he's about to be a dad, but even more thoughts go through his head when he finds out that he is having a daughter. This reality can chase even the strongest man away from his responsibility. Not knowing how to handle his emotions and control his thoughts can deceive a man into believing that his child will be better off if he's not around. And that's a deception of perception. Being the father of 4 girls, I can relate. And that's one of the reasons why I wrote this book.

As fathers, we know what our daughters are up against. We know how the world talks and what beautiful pictures the world can paint that will draw our daughters' attention. Our only downfall as men is that most of us can't express our true thoughts clearly to our daughters without our emotions getting in the way.

When most men feel fear, anger rises up. Men hate to lose, so when we believe our daughters are in or headed in a compromising position with a boy, friends, or people at school, fear rises up, causing us to get angry at the situation and not at our daughter. And when our daughters question us, we feel that they're questioning our advice and our authority. Fear for them going in the wrong direction rises up because we see our innocent daughters and a mean ol' world.

When our little girls ask questions like:

- » When can I get a phone?
- » When can I get a boyfriend?
- » When can I start going to parties?

Or make statements like:

- » I want a phone!
- » I want a boyfriend!
- » I want to go to a party!

We go into panic mode and become uneasy like Anger in the animated movie "Inside Out." Dads go into what I call "The Anger Mode" when our authority is being questioned by anyone who can't see the trouble that we see up ahead. When our daughters have an "I don't see what's the big deal" attitude and turn away from us, ready to walk off into a bad situation, not caring about their dad's wisdom or input on the subject, a sense of rejection rises up inside of us, and the only way we know to express how we feel is to look and be angry, have short conversations, or avoid the entire situation altogether. None of those options are healthy for any relationship, especially between a dad and his daughter. The main problem in this situation is that our little girls are growing up **and we're not ready for it...** and we don't believe that they are as ready as they believe they are.

My hope is that dads and daughters can stay on common ground and understand each other. I don't want the girl who sees her dad's anger to think:

- » He doesn't like me.
- » He's mad at me.
- » He doesn't care about me.
- » He's embarrassed by me.

He does like you. He's just having a hard time processing his thoughts. He's angry at himself and the situation. He's angry at himself because he's having a hard time explaining the dangers of the situation to you, when you are so eager to go into a situation where you have no idea of what's really going on. He's angry at the situation because he believes if you could "only" see what he sees, you wouldn't walk into the situation so willingly without asking more questions in order to become more informed. Because he's the dad, he will see things that you won't see, so he has the obligation of saying **NO** when everyone else is saying **YES** because they don't see with "daddy eyes." He knows you just want what you want and aren't considering all that is at stake. Dads have to learn how to handle this emotion and try to talk to their daughters with love, while being honest and truthful.

Another thing we as dads hope our daughters know is that we still love them in spite of how they may see our relationship with their mom.

Most dads hope their daughters grow up to be better than their mom and marry a man better than their dad. That's not to knock either of us down; it's just a fact. Most men prefer that their daughters:

» Accomplish more in life.
» Avoid mistakes.
» Live a purer life than they did.

We as parents hope that our daughters end up with a good man who will love and take care of them as a good man should and that they will be good to him as well. Every dad knows what another man is willing to deal with or tolerate, so we hope to teach our daughters how to be smart and not "freely-kneely" because if a woman lives carefree with no plans for life and no rules, standards, or boundaries, then she will continue to live "freely-kneely" when married or in a serious relationship. This will continue until she either learns to do right on her own or is taught to do right by someone else.

I believe that in order for a daughter not to live "freely-kneely", dads have to stand up and teach their daughters (and their sons) standards. But until then, I want to inform you that your dad does have a hope for you, and he does love you, even though he may not be able to explain it to you.

I also want you to know that your dad will always want to have a healthy relationship with you, even if he and your mom don't. Relationships are hard, and not every relationship makes it. So, if your parents' relationship isn't the best, and things aren't as good as you want them to be, remember that what happens between your parents isn't because of you. Things don't always work out as they should or how we would prefer them to, and for some people it seems easier to give up and let the other person win than to fight and make a mess of things.

In those instances, I want to apologize to you on behalf of dads so that you don't think their relationship is the norm or that you will be the same way when you grow up. Here is my apology:

_____(Your name here), I want to apologize for all the times you wanted me there with you and I wasn't._____ (Your name here), I want to apologize for all the fussing and fighting and awkward moments that your mom and I had either on the phone or face to face around you that no child should have had to endure.

_____(Your name here), I'm sorry for not hugging you when you needed it. I'm sorry for not being the man you needed me to be. _____(Your name here), I want to apologize for everything.

~ NOW READ IT AGAIN BEFORE YOU MOVE ON ~

Life has more important stuff to focus on without us holding on to past events. You are wonderfully and fearfully made. You are a wonderful girl. I hope you can forgive those that have hurt your feelings. I hope you can grow and be happy with yourself. If you need to read the apology again, please do. And once you have forgiven, move forward and ask God to help you rebuild your faith in people. It may be a slow go, but it's important to get it done. I hope you know that you can be and do more in life. So, as you continue on your journey of hope, let's stay focused and explore more of a dad's hope.

Daily Journal

Today is _____   The time is _____
I am _____

Daddy Daughter Discussion Section

TOPIC _____

CHAPTER 2

A DAD'S HOPE THAT HIS DAUGHTER DON'T

Not all, but many of the dads I know have a hope for their daughters to be different. It's a feeling, sensing, and desire we as men have deep down inside of us for our children, especially for our girls. We want them to be different and not like the crowd or their friends.

The world can be a hard place, especially for good girls, and every dad wants his daughter to strive to be a good girl. Not perfect, but good. Not flawless, but good. Not even a "Miss Goodie-Two-Shoes," just a girl that is good at being herself and holding her own.

"How do I become that?" you may be asking. I believe it all starts by knowing the truth about the women in your family, about how the world is set up for women, and about yourself.

Let me use myself and the men in my family as an example. There are three things that have stunted the growth of the men in my family: drinking, smoking, and chasing women. The men in my family that drink and smoke have a shorter lifespan than the men who don't. The men in my family that smoke and drink have worse relationship problems than the men who don't. And the men that use and abuse women have terrible relationship issues that prevent them from fulfilling their purpose because they don't have a woman to help them.

You may be thinking, of course if a man drinks, smokes, and uses women, he will obviously have those problems. Statistics say that will happen. But let me tell you that is not true for all men. As a little boy, I heard this truth because there are two parts to every man: the momma side and the daddy side. The men on my mom side is different from the men on my dad's, and the men on my dad side is different from my mom's. They may have similar problems, but they handle their problems differently.

I say all that to ask you, what's in your family? Do you know? Do you know that your dad knows, and he has a hope for you not to act out what may be inside of you?

As a dad, I hope my daughters make the better choice. I know what's inside of them, and I pray and hope they make right decisions. I believe your dad has the same hope for you. No matter how old you are right now, your dad wants the best for you, even if you don't believe he does. Again, I want you to know that it's hard for him to say it and express it.

I want to take a quick pause and say that I may not know your current situation with your dad or your current perceptions about yourself. But I do pray that you believe me. I know that, as a man, I'll never understand what a girl may go through. But as a dad, I have hope that you won't have to go through unnecessary experiences. As a dad, I wish I could take all the molesters, rapists, heart breakers, child abusers, and women beaters away, but I can't. What I can do is stand up and say, "Hey dads, we need to do better."

I can watch and listen to women like Joyce Meyer, who was abused by her dad when she was young, and hope for the best for other girls. I'm sure that there are many more women out there with similar stories. But my hope is for you. That you find help in your hurt or talk to your dad or mom about the women in your family. I also want to warn you that many women are ashamed of their past, so they may not want to share this information with you. If that's the case, recognize that they won't tell you and just pay attention to your aunties and grandmas. See how their lives ended up: what made them a successful or not so successful woman and what got them to where they are, either good or bad in your sight.

I am saying all this because I know and have seen how the world, TV, and Internet portray people. As a dad, it can make me a little scared for my girls. The world can pressure dads to lower the standard for our daughters because of the way the world is, and that's not acceptable. As a dad who believes in God, I can't do that, so I'm not going to do that. Therefore, I will hope. And I hope you will, too. Times are changing. We live in a world where it's easy to exchange our hope for the world's hope. Let's make a movement to keep hope alive for ourselves and for our families.

Daily Journal

TODAY IS _____ THE TIME IS _____

I AM _____

Daddy Daughter Discussion Section

Topic

Chapter 3

Hope You Hope

A DAD'S HOPE FOR HIS DAUGHTER TO HOPE

In this chapter, we will be talking about a dad's hope for his daughter to have her own ambitions and her own hopes and dreams that have not been contaminated by the world's view on life or how her life should be.

Ever since she was a little girl, my wife, Robyn, always knew that she wanted to be a wife and mother. She didn't know what job she wanted or where she wanted to live, but she did know that marriage and parenthood were important to her. And I believe that since she wanted that at an early age, that is the reason why she has a husband and five incredible children. As a dad and a husband, I want to encourage my daughters and other girls to have the same courage to go after what they want as well.

Don't accept, expect, or transform into the world's way of thinking or doing things just because everyone else is doing it. You are your own person with your own life to live. There are "right ways" and "wrong ways" in life, but you don't have to:

- » Conform to this just because you're "Black"
- » Be like this because you're "White"
- » Act like this because you're Biracial, Hispanic, Asian, or whatever God has blessed you to be.

Be you, and be happy with that. You are one of God greatest creations -- a woman. God has graced you to be an original, one-of-a-kind. For my wife, God gave her the dream and desire to be a wife and mother at an early age. What is God showing you now that He wants for you? Think about what you want out of life. What is that dream you can't seem to shake or forget about? If God hasn't shown it to you yet, keep looking because He will. Pay attention to yourself. God created you, and you're special. In my wife's book Fulfilment, she talks about how being happy with who you are and doing what you are called by God to do is so fulfilling, so never forget or let the world take your personality away because it wants you to fit into a category that was not made for you. You will never fit comfortably into a box that the world wants to put you in, so don't even try, no matter what other people may tell you. Just be the original girl God created you to be.

He knew you before He formed you in your mother's womb. Before you were born He set you apart and appointed you as my prophet to the nations.
Jeremiah 1:5 (NLT)

Daily Journal

TODAY IS _____ THE TIME IS _____

I AM _____

Daddy Daughter Discussion Section

TOPIC _____

CHAPTER 4

Hope You Believe

A DAD'S HOPE FOR HIS DAUGHTER TO BELIEVE

As a God-fearing dad and a Christian man, I want my daughters to believe in a power higher than themselves and those around them. I want them to be able to see and get more out of life than just what's going on with Snap Chat, Facebook, Instagram, ect. I want them to be able to look up and see life for what it is and not only how life looks through their phones.

As a dad I want them to be able to think on their own and make decisions on their own based on what they have been taught by their mom and me. If that's not enough, I want them to have the ability to hear that still, small voice within themselves called the Holy Spirit. I'm aware that there are those who don't believe in the possibility of hearing the

Holy Spirit, but as a Christian, I believe it's there for anyone who believes. God gave the Holy Spirit to:

- » Comfort us when we're hurt and alone,
- » Help us when making decisions,
- » Teach us to have good judgment, and
- » Lead us in all truth when we don't know which way to go in life.

It's been given to us by God Himself. I'm not trying to force my religion and beliefs about God on anyone, but I will say that it's there for the taking for anyone who believes. Here are the advantages and disadvantages of having the Holy Spirit and not having the Holy Spirit.

Having a Holy Spirit Led Life

But the Holy Spirit produces this kind of fruit in our lives:
- Love
- Joy
- Peace
- Patience
- Kindness
- Goodness
- Faithfulness
- Gentleness
- Self-Control

There is no law against these things!
Gal 5:22-23 (NLT)

Having a Flesh Led Life

When you follow the desires of your sinful nature, the results are very clear:
- Sexual Immorality
- Impurity
- Lustful Pleasures
- Idolatry
- Sorcery
- Hostility
- Quarreling
- Jealousy
- Outbursts of Anger
- Selfish Ambition
- Dissension
- Division
- Envy
- Drunkenness
- Wild Parties

And other sins like these. Let me tell you again, as I have before, that anyone living that sort of life will not inherit the Kingdom of God.
Gal 5:19-21 (NLT)

The world is full of people doing their own thing and believing in only what they want to believe. As a dad I want you to believe in what is right and Biblically correct and not what is politically and socially correct. Dare to believe in what is unbelievable to the world.

Daily Journal

TODAY IS _____ THE TIME IS _____

I AM _____

Daddy Daughter Discussion Section

TOPIC _____

CHAPTER 5

Hope You See

A DAD'S HOPE FOR HIS DAUGHTER TO SEE

In this chapter we will be going over how your dad sees your virginity, sex, and boys. Let's start with **virginity.**

According to the Webster Dictionary, virginity means the unmarried or celibate life. VIRGINITY by daddy's definition means you stay my little angel; not having sex EVER, not even in marriage. Adopt a kid or get a pet and name it "Daddy"; never think about sex, hear about sex, learn about sex, or even find out about sex ever, never ever, never ever, never ever. Boys are bad. ☺ Ewwwww, boys.

Oh how we wish it was that easy.
But it can't be, so we must continue

This is how most dads see sex, boys, and love when it comes to their daughters. I have placed a story from a good friend of mine in this section of the book to give it a motherly touch. It explains how she was once around your age and how she wishes things would have turned out if only she would have had someone explain the truth about boys and all that comes with being a girl your age.

> If you're a dad, this story may make you cringe. If you're a daughter, ask your dad why it makes him cringe. Dads, please explain to your daughters how you think my friend could have avoided this situation, and how you hope your daughter avoids the same thing.

The Mirage

My Friend's Story

My moment happened in 4th grade when I had one of my first "boyfriends". He was cute, with curly hair and a deeper-than-normal 4th grade boy's voice. We used to sit on top of the monkey bars, and he would let me wear his jacket. Then it ended when he got a new girlfriend, and I got a new "boyfriend."

Fast forward to high school.

That Night

It all started with an invitation to a party. A guy friend invited me to his birthday party, which was supposed to be at his house. My parents knew his mom, so it was approved for me to go. My sister would drive me and my best friend to the party. Simple enough, right?

Then BOOM, I ended up sitting in a car with him during the party, and I was that young girl again with a big crush on a memory of a 4th grade "relationship".

After that encounter, it was like things just moved along by themselves. There were notes passed to me and phone calls made to me. Texting and sexting didn't exist back then. I didn't have to do anything. We talked that night at the party, then we were together the next week at school. He was telling me he loved me maybe a couple of weeks to a month after that. All I saw was how much he needed me and how much he said he couldn't make it without me.

Other People's Delusions

Others can amplify the effects of the mirage. I had mutual friends telling me about how much I was helping him and how he was becoming a better person because of me. Side Note: he was a heavy "smoker" (not of cigarettes). These "cigarettes" had not been made legal in the state of Alabama yet. So of course, me being the good girl I was, I saw myself as the tool God was going to use to save this boy. (Granted, God had never told me this, and I don't even remember talking to God about Him "using me" to do anything for this boy. This was all me, but even in these times in our lives, God will still love us through a mirage and even work things out for our good despite what we do.)

This boy would go to church with me and come sit at my house with me on the weekends, which meant he wasn't out there "smoking" right? Or at least not as much. At least that's what I saw because I wanted to see it. I wanted to see that he was better, that I was helping him to be better. That if I could just stay with him, he would stop "smoking" and do better in school and develop a relationship with God. That's a lot to ask of a 16 year old girl, but I just knew that I could do it. I wanted to see those things. They were not real, but they seemed so real to me in the moment, which is exactly what mirages are. They're a trick of the eye where you see something that isn't there.

He gave me a note that had a conversation between him and one of my close female friends, where he was asking her to "give him some" but she refused. I later found out that he thought he gave me a note inviting me to a cookout with his family. He asked me later why I had not responded to the note about the cookout. I was clueless, and he was clueless until I put the two things together. But I stayed. I didn't leave. I didn't ask any questions. I just stayed and acted like nothing had happened.

It was like in a movie when you know if someone would just say something or do something, the outcome of the story would be different. Well, that was my moment, and I did nothing. I was still believing in the mirage of true love and a happy ending. Hoping I could change it into something that it wasn't. I thought I could change him, make him want to be what I hoped he could be and not just the weed-smoking, girl-playing guy that everyone knew he was and expected him to be and what he really wanted to be. You see, it wasn't my purpose, position, or responsibility to take care of and change a teenage boy. It was a mirage and not reality.

I had plenty of opportunities to walk away from that relationship that would lead to my pregnancy. Young girls, 99.7% of the time there is a way out, and you can walk away or stop everything from happening. I broke up with the guy twice before I decided to have sex with him. Even after "almost" walking away and preventing the whole thing from happening, I still stayed. I still got pregnant. I spent the second semester of my senior year pregnant. I couldn't participate in the main Miss High School pageant. I couldn't participate in Senior Skip Day. I couldn't play in the final basketball game of my high school career.

When I decided to do that thing that I knew was not in God's best interest for me (that whole free will thing that we as humans have), I missed out on what should have been that happiest and most fun-filled time of my high school life. Oh yeah, I didn't mention the college scholarship I lost. A Scholarship with full tuition, room and board, and full coverage for books was gone out the window of my life because I believed and wanted something that didn't exist.

Because I saw "helping" this guy as being more valuable than keeping my virginity, I lost it. I just gave it away and couldn't get it back. Like I've said before, the mirage can make you see things that aren't really there. Because, you see, a mirage is not only what you see but also what you

DON'T see. I saw a guy who needed me, a guy who said he loved me, and I thought I was the only one who could help him. All I had to do was give this precious thing to him, and he could become the man he needed to be to succeed in life. By seeing him as the one in need, I also stopped looking at my virginity as something valuable enough to keep and not give away. I know this sounds ridiculous, but many women have put themselves in the same type of situation at least once. God created us to be helpers to man. That is what comes naturally to us, I believe. In our most fragile and naïve states -- our teenage years -- that's what we gravitate toward doing. That is why it is so critical for fathers and daughters to have relationships where they talk to each other. Mothers also need to stay as close as possible to their daughters during this time. This is the time when girls are most vulnerable to being tricked by boys and the ways of the world. Daughters, you **HAVE** to listen to your mothers. And if your mother isn't talking, find your dad. God didn't allow us parents to go through the things we've gone through just to sit on all that wisdom and not talk about it with our children. Girls, daughters, listen to what your parents have to tell you. They've been there before, they've seen it, they've lost it, they've regretted it, and deep down inside, they don't want you to do the same. I'm not saying all mothers have been fooled by boys and men, but the women I know can relate.

As parents we **HAVE** to talk to our daughters in order to help them to stay away from the mistakes we have made. We must teach them to not believe in the ways of the world. Dads **MUST** tell their daughters the truth in order for them to stay off that path and not be consumed by the world. They must tell them the truth about boys and how they, their friends, and boys they knew treated girls. We must pray to God that they hear our words. It's hard to share that part of our lives because it may be embarrassing or hurtful, and we don't want to look back to the past, but for the sake of our daughters' futures, we have to. They need us to, even if they don't know it yet. Daughters out there need to hear what we know so that they can see more clearly. So that they can see what might happen before someone tries to trick them into doing something wrong.

Your virginity is a very precious thing that most people (men and women) take for granted. With mine, there was never even a question about it. I would keep mine until I got married. I made up in my mind that I would not have sex before marriage. I had no desire for sex. I didn't even think about sex when I saw it on T.V. But because I didn't talk to the right people, and I didn't understand the little that I knew, I gave up a part of myself that I should not have given up so soon. Value your virginity. And even if you don't have it anymore, value yourself. Have a hope for yourself that the world doesn't have.

BACK TO BEN

My friend told me this story a long time ago, and I thought to myself, all she needed was someone to tell her the truth. That was it. Like she said, she was determined to keep her virginity until marriage, but someone else told her something that changed her perception, and she believed it. As a dad, that's heartbreaking because I believe she needed a man telling her that what she had was valuable and that she needed to keep it for the husband who would come one day. I know that this might seem impossible in this day and age, but I believe in the impossible.

SEX

Having sex with a boy is a big deal. Sex is meant for a man and woman who are married. Today's society will tell you different, but it's still Biblically true. Even some Christians have changed their standards on this because they are ashamed of their pasts and have watered virginity down to a dilute substance. They say, "If you can keep it then good for you, but if you can't, God's grace will cover that for you." That is true, but as a dad, I want to raise the standard of virginity for our children. I tell my daughters, "I'm not expecting you to be perfect because there's no such thing as a perfect person, so relax. I just want you to be perfectly you. You have too much of me and your mommy in you to be perfect, anyway."

For the young lady who is reading this book, be yourself, but know that there's a time and place for everything. Don't rush into sex because of a boy, your friends, or what the world is telling you.

BOYS

Believe it or not, your dad was a boy at one time in his life. As dads who were boys that became men, we understand how boys think, how they act, and why they want what they want.

There are 2 popular sayings about boys.
1. They only want one thing.
2. They are all the same.

Unfortunately, they're both true in men's opinions (Mainly when it comes to our daughters, of course). When it comes to boyfriends and boys that are friends, you have to be clear on what you are dealing with because there's a difference. Boys who are friends are just boys that like to see you in school or say hey to you at a game or any other school-related social event. But a "boyfriend" between the ages of 12 to 16 only wants to do that one thing: have sex or anything similar to sex. Here are some differences between boys that are friends and boyfriends:

- » Boys who are friends say, "Hey, how are you doing," "It's good to see you" kind of stuff.
- » Boyfriends may say the same thing, but they're thinking things like, "Hey, what can I do to you that won't make you feel too uncomfortable" or "It would be good to see you naked one day."
- » Boys who are friends will open doors for you.
- » Boyfriends will close doors behind you to get you alone.

With these sayings, "They're all the same" and "They only want one thing," different types of boys have different ways to getting what they want, which is sex, or anything related to sex. One boyfriend is patient and willing to wait for a certain moment to get what he wants. Another type of boyfriend will pretty much let you know up front what he wants just by the way he talks to you and acts around you.

Dads hate this type of boyfriend because he's disrespecting our daughters in front of us, and she seems to either be ok with it or doesn't believe that the way he's acting is wrong, which makes a dad even more upset because his daughter is being duped.

It always helps us as dads to know that our daughters trust our judgment and listen to us. Now, let's stop right here and discuss this chapter. I hope you've learned something new. In the daily journal section of this book, you and your dad or mom or friends should discuss what you've just read.

Here are 3 strategies that will help daughters gain understanding of what their dads are telling them.

1. Understand that your dad has no reason to lie to you in this situation.
    a. Take a moment and take your eyes off the thing you want and listen. Put your phone away and take a walk down the road or in the park with your dad.
2. Realize that you may not be seeing the full picture.
    b. Ask someone, "What do you see? How do you see this playing out for me?"
3. Ask yourself, "Why do I really want to (blank)?"
    c. If you're still in the moment of wanting to do or have whatever it is that you want without a reason, repeat steps 1 and 2 until your mind is clear and you're not in your feelings.

Daily Journal

TODAY IS_____ THE TIME IS_____
I AM_____

Daddy Daughter Discussion Section

Topic

CHAPTER 6

Hope You Grow

A DAD'S HOPE FOR HIS DAUGHTER TO GROW

As a dad, I want my daughters to grow spiritually into women of purpose, physically into women of class, and mentally into women of high standard.

If my daughters are easily discouraged, I want them to think, "Hey, why am I being an ol' stick in the mud. I am wonderfully and fearfully made. I can't stay like this."

If my daughters love eating and have noticed that they are a little heavier than they would prefer to be, I want them to be like, "Hey, I am wonderfully and fearfully made. I can't stay like this."

And if she feels like she's missing something on the inside of herself, I want her to say, "Hey God, thank you for making me wonderfully and fearfully. Because of you, I don't have to feel like this."

I will praise thee; for I am fearfully and wonderfully made: marvelous are thy works; and that my soul knoweth right well. Psalms 139:14 KJV

I know you are going to have a bunch of mixed emotions. We all do. But I want you to understand that God has made us all wonderfully and fearfully, and we don't have to "stay" in our feelings. We can get out of them.

We don't have to think that no one else "gets me" like my friends do. God "gets you," and your parents do too, but they may not "accept it" like your friends do because they know that you can be better. If they comfort you where you are, you may not want to get out of the funk that you're in.

God understands, and He will love you no matter where you are, but your parents are there to:

1. Guide you out of where you are.
2. Pull you out of where you are or help you.
3. Wait until you see that you can get out, once you get over your feelings.

Dads hate to see their children mentally, physically, or spiritually defeated. It does something to us on the inside that makes us angry. As men, we want our words to work for you. When we say "stop", "go", "no" or "yes", we expect things to change. If I say, "we'll see" or "maybe so" to my kids, I expect them to wait with expectation or anticipation and not be like "this will never happen."

As a father, I want to speak to you as a daughter and tell you that life may not be exactly like you prefer it to be, but you are still here, and there is a lot of growing up you have to do. Be patient. Learn to recognize and control your emotions. Learn how to talk about your emotions so you can explain and understand what is really going on with you.

There are more people who care about you than you think. You're more important than you know, and you're prettier than you believe. Life may not be exactly like you want it to be, but it's not over. Time is passing, TV shows are still coming on, stores are still open, and there are 4 more chapters to read. Keep going, and don't get in a funk.

Life is what you make it. You may be facing new problems at school and experiencing new emotions in your body, but you are in control of it, and you've got this. Love, Laugh, Live, Go and Grow.

You created every part of me; you put me together in my mother's womb. (Psalms 139:13 GNB)

As a man thinketh, so is he.

As a girl laugheth, so is she.

As a dog barketh, the cat runneth.

Eeny, meeny, miny, moe.

Catch a tiger by its toe.

If it hollers let it go.

Eeny, meeny, miny, moe.

My momma told me to pick you, so you are it.

That makes no sense. But you do.

Go out and be great. ☺

Daily Journal

TODAY IS _____ THE TIME IS _____

I AM _____

Daddy Daughter Discussion Section

TOPIC: What do you want to grow into?

CHAPTER 7

Hope You Love

A DAD'S HOPE FOR HIS DAUGHTER TO LOVE

I believe the secret ingredient to life is love. I believe we should mix it into everything we do. We should mix love into:

- » The way we interact with people.
- » How we take care of ourselves.
- » Even in the way we cook our food.

It's always a good idea to mix a measure of love in everything we do because the things we remember the most all have a measure of love connected to them. No matter if it's a hug, a song, a gift, or a meal with family and friends, it has a measure of love somewhere in it that made it memorable. Love is the most powerful ingredient. The Bible describes love like this:

**Love is patient and kind. Love is not jealous or boastful or proud or rude. It does not demand its own way. It is not irritable, and it keeps no record of being wronged. It does not rejoice about injustice but rejoices whenever the truth wins out. Love never gives up, never loses faith, is always hopeful, and endures through every circumstance.
1 Corinthians 13:4-7 (NLT)**

Love can literally change the outcome of an event. I know we all have bad memories as well, but I also believe that with the right amount, Love can replace and take away those bad memories and give a different perspective of the past.

As a dad, I want you to know that it makes a dad happy to know that his daughter has the capability to love herself, and one day her husband and her kids. I know that you have a long time to worry about that, since you're a kid, but dads look at our girls and wonder "how will she be when she has a life of her own? What do I need to help her with in order for her to get it? I hope she will be better than her mom and I are. I hope she does a better job taking care of her kids than I do. I hope she finds a man that can love her better than I can. I hope she has a better relationship with God than I have."

Even if you're 9, 5, 12, 14, 17, or 2, your dad sees it. We look at our girls and have all kinds of thoughts. What about this? What about that? What would she do if she had this? Can she do this? I wonder if she knows about this. I wonder if she knows about that. I hope she doesn't find some no-good joker that will ruin her life. I hope she knows how to love herself and do as the Bible says and love her husband, kids, and God because He first loved her.

WAYS TO PRAY

Here is one way my mom taught me to pray when I was younger:

> Lord, thank you for my family. I pray that you take care of them and keep them safe. Now, Lord, I pray that you take care of me and make me whole in Jesus' name.

You can talk to God anyway you like, just as if He was a friend or if you were in a room talking to yourself.

This is the Lord's Prayer found in Matthew 6:9-13 of the Bible:

Our Father which art in heaven,

Hallowed be thy name.

Thy kingdom come. Thy will be done in earth, as it is in heaven.

Give us this day our daily bread.

And forgive us our debts, as we forgive our debtors.

And lead us not into temptation, but deliver us from evil: For thine is the kingdom, and the power, and the glory, for ever. Amen.

As a dad, I hope you grow in love.

Daily Journal

TODAY IS _____ THE TIME IS _____
I AM _____

Daddy Daughter Discussion Section

Topic _____

CHAPTER 8
~~Hope You~~ Understand

A DAD'S HOPE FOR HIS DAUGHTER TO UNDERSTAND

I'm sure you have noticed that I mention "the world" a lot throughout this book. As dads, it's our job to inform our children about the ways of the world and the games that can be played by people in the world. The Bible says in Romans 12:2:

Don't copy the behavior and customs of this world, but let God transform you into a new person by changing the way you think. Then you will learn to know God's will for you, which is good and pleasing and perfect. Romans 12:2 (NLT)

The world is a very deceptive place, influenced by a lower power called Satan. I'm not trying to scare you or force my religion on you but inform you. The Bible says in II Corinthians 4:4 that:

Satan, who is the god of this world, has blinded the minds of those who don't believe. They are unable to see the glorious light of the Good News. They don't understand this message about the glory of Christ, who is the exact likeness of God. 2 Corinthians 4:4 (NLT)

This may seem to be a lot information for where you are in life right now, but as a dad, I want you to know. I want you to be aware of the things that will try to suck you in and change the trajectory of your life. Daughter, your dad has seen some things in his life that he doesn't want you to have to go through and experience. And really, we see things every day that we want our children to be aware of, so they won't get drawn in and used for evil.

We want our children to understand that everything seen on TV or watched on the internet or told by friends isn't what it may appear to be. This is not limited to what is seen but also includes people, mainly boys.

There are good people out there in entertainment land, too. The Internet can even be used as a powerful and great tool that can improve our daily lives, but as a dad, I want you to be aware of the things that are damaging to your future and know the things that aren't respectable to you. I'm sure you're a very smart girl, and that's great, but it's a dad's job to keep you away from bad stuff. We're also here to keep you away from a lot of stuff you may want to experience sooner than you are ready, like phones, boys, no-good friends, and some of the other things that we have already discussed in this book.

I want you to know that it pleases us dads to know that our girls "got this." They've got this thing called life under control and are not being controlled by it. They're not influenced by what they see and don't believe that if they don't have what what's-a-name has (make-up, clothes, and things of that nature) that their lives suck. It upsets us as men to think that we didn't send our girls out prepared. It frustrates us to know that we tried to prepare our children, but they refused to listen. It depresses us to know we couldn't teach our children everything we know because we didn't know how to communicate with our daughters, and now they're subject to the influence of the world.

If you're 10 or older, I'm sure you have caught on to this by now just by what you have seen on TV or the Internet. It makes dads happy to know that our daughters understand life and the ways of the world, and if she doesn't fully understand, she's willing to ask her dad for help, wisdom, and understanding. If she's not willing to talk with her dad, she should have good friends that will tell her the truth and give her wisdom that will help her make wise decisions.

Things to Know About the Bible

The Bible describes wisdom as a woman. Please check this out:

Don't turn your back on wisdom, for she will protect you. Love her, and she will guard you. Getting wisdom is the wisest thing you can do! And whatever else you do, develop good judgment. Proverbs 4:6-7 (NLT)

As a dad who wants a good relationship with his daughters, I understand that it can be hard for some dads to voice their opinion to their daughters. You have this grown man trying to explain to this young lady that she doesn't need to do what everyone else is doing. One thing that makes this so hard for dads is that the world (TV and the internet) is making everything look so acceptable these days. It makes it seem OK for girls to wear that, or go there, and do that with them, or be called out of their name as if they don't care to respect themselves or care if anyone else respects them either, but as a dad who cares about your future, I'm telling you that it's not OK for you to do whatever it is you may think you want to do because of what you see. And that's not just for you, that's for anyone. We should listen to what the Bible says in 1 Corinthians 6:12:

"I have the right to do anything," you say – but not everything is beneficial. I have the right to do anything – but I will not be mastered by anything.

That means yes, there's a lot of stuff that is available to us, but we don't have to partake of it just because it's available to us. Not wanting or going after everything that's available will take discipline. The world is an inviting place. It does a great job tempting us to come into it, but as a dad, I want you to be informed and stand strong against the ways of the world. You're too precious and important to be used for anything less than who you are.

Wisdom is the principal thing; *Therefore,* get wisdom. And in all your getting, get understanding. Proverbs 4:7 (NKJV)

And now on a deeper note...

Your Parents' Relationship

This section is for the girl whose parents are together but not doing very well, and she can tell. To you I want to say that it's ok to feel the way you do, if you feel bad at all.

Just don't let it get the best of you. You may be thinking, "How can I not? They're my parents."

You may or may not understand why things aren't going like you would like them to be, but I want to tell you from a dad's perspective that you will always be daddy's little girl. I know that it may be heartbreaking, life-changing, and future-dictating when your parents are not together, or they're together but not involved in your life, or they're fighting all the time, or one has passed away before their time. Trying to understand the "why" of "grown up people stuff" is hard, but as a man and a dad, I've noticed that some dads just aren't up for the challenge. Are you worth it? Yes! Can he do it? Yes and No. For some men, dealing with the mother of their children is hard. It's the same for women. They may have a hard time dealing with the fathers of their children, so it's easier to just give up and stay away.

I am not trying to justify your parents' actions at all or pick one side over the other; I'm just letting you know that trying to understand adult relationships at your age may not make much sense. But understanding that you don't have to end up like them is possible. You can start preparing yourself for life now by watching the lives of others and learning about what's in you, so you'll know what to avoid when you get older. Believe in a higher power and be aware that there is a lower power working for the world that is ready to pull you into his way of thinking by getting you caught up in a life of lies and foolish thinking. As a dad, I hope you know that you're worth more than the value the world may put on you, and I hope you take this information as advice and not as commands or condemnation. I hope you understand.

Daily Journal

TODAY IS _____ THE TIME IS _____

I AM _____

Daddy Daughter Discussion Section

TOPIC

CHAPTER 9
I Hope You See What I See

A DAD'S HOPE FOR HIS DAUGHTER TO SEE WHAT HE SEES

When a man looks at his daughter, he sees the most precious gift a man can have. He sees a beautiful girl that will one day become a beautiful woman. As a dad of four beauty queens, I believe other men can relate when I say I see a little bit of my mom, my sisters, my aunties, and my grandmothers, and a whole lot of their mother in them. We see all of our favorite people embedded in one person, and that's you, precious daughter.

If your dad is around, and you can get in touch with him, I encourage you to ask him what he sees. Tell him you're reading a book, and you want to know what he thinks when he looks at you. Tell him his answer is important to you. He might be uncomfortable, so don't expect him to answer right away. Give him some time to put it into words, and he'll respond when he can. If your dad isn't around, and you can't get in contact with him, here's what your Heavenly Father says about you:

For we you are God's handiwork created in Christ Jesus to do good works which God prepared in advance for us to do

Ephesians 2:10

You are the salt of the earth

Matthew 5:13

You are the light of the world

Matthew 5:14

For the sake of his great name the Lord will not reject his people you because the Lord was pleased to make you his own

1Samuel 12:22

You're loved more than you know and by now I'm hoping you're starting to realize it. I hope you see what I've been saying.

Before you were formed in your mother's womb I (I as in God) knew you, before you were born I (I as in God) set you apart. Jeremiah 1:5

Daily Journal

TODAY IS _____ THE TIME IS _____

I AM _____

Daddy Daughter Discussion Section

TOPIC

Chapter 10

A DAD'S HOPE FOR HIS DAUGHTER TO BE

Be happy, be successful, be authentic, be genuine, and most of all, be YOURSELF. This is how most dads want their daughters to be. My prayer for you is that you have gained an understanding about your dad, your mom, and yourself by reading this book. I hope you have taken good notes throughout this book so that you can go back over your notes and reflect and realize how your life was at this time. As time goes by, you can monitor your growth through what you wrote in these pages as proof of your changing.

I hope that you are happy with yourself and are focused on what you might want to change because you are a great daughter, despite how you may see yourself. You're growing up. We all are -- even adults. Who you are this year will more than likely be different than who you will be in two years if you decide to continue to grow.

- » The way you see...
- » What you believe...
- » The friends you pick...

...will change if you remember what you have read in this book and don't settle for the belief that life will always be like this, so why try.

In Conclusion

As we come to an end, let this be the beginning of your discovery -- the discovery of who you are and what you hope for. I hope you know that there's a higher power out there than what's being advertised. I hope and pray that you make this book personal and grow from it. As a dad of four girls, I hope I was able to make this journey relatable, amusing, eye opening, door closing, and life changing for you, your dad, and everyone you know. Keep this book of HOPE always.

To my four daughters: if I haven't said it enough, I love you. Despite the frowns, the fear, the frustration, and the joy on my face you see day by day, I love you and I always will. To the rest of you Gifts from God, take care and take it easy.

With much love,
Ben

Daily Journal

Today is _____ The time is _____

I am _____

Daddy Daughter Discussion Section

TOPIC

www.ingramcontent.com/pod-product-compliance
Lightning Source LLC
Chambersburg PA
CBHW071725040426
42446CB00011B/2220